PIERO MANZONI

THE TWIN PAINTINGS

Hauser & Wirth Publishers
Fondazione Piero Manzoni

FOREWORD
Rosalia Pasqualino di Marineo

Extraordinary events for those who, like me, run a foundation, do not happen too often: the opening of a major exhibition, the publication of a wonderful biography, the presentation of a documentary on the artist . . . moments of satisfaction, and emotion, that result from the many days of hard work, the laying of one brick after another in the months and years that came before, the delicate threads woven before that have nothing to do—when examined individually—with the spark of the final event.

The project featuring these two *Achromes*, "heterozygous twins," is definitely something out of the ordinary. Actually, for me it is probably a unique occurrence and one that is unlikely to be repeated: two such important paintings, different and yet the same, which could be placed side by side and studied once again and more in-depth this time, thanks to the great interest that Hauser & Wirth has shown in scholarly research. An irregularly creased canvas and a stitched one, both of them with extensive use of kaolin. One of the two works has already been exhibited in many prestigious exhibitions, whereas the other has been hidden from public view until not long ago. Two canvases of such extraordinary force, capable of taking my breath away the first time I saw them together in a room in Zurich, in the company of the authors of the texts you will read in this book.

So this is a precious moment, and the following pages are special ones too, for which I certainly wish to thank the three authors of the texts, together with everyone at Hauser & Wirth who collaborated, with professionalism and sincere enthusiasm, in the presentation of these stunning twin *Achromes*.

Rosalia Pasqualino di Marineo
Director, Fondazione Piero Manzoni

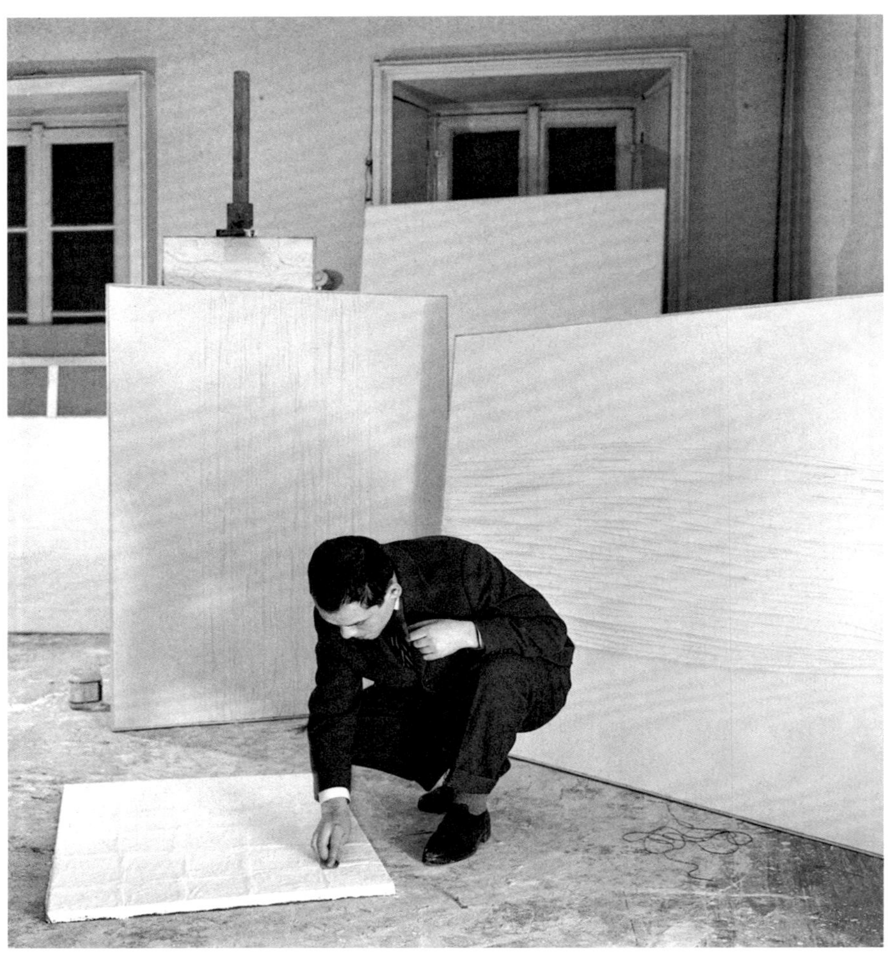

Manzoni in his atelier on Via Fiori Oscuri, Milan, 1958

PIERO MANZONI:
THE IDEA OF THE ACHROME
Flaminio Gualdoni

"We cannot accept any manifestation of color that is meant to be a medium," wrote Piero Manzoni in his theoretical text *Una nuova zona di immagini* (A New Zone of Images). The year was 1957, and Manzoni was working on his first *Achromes*. Early the following year, the critic and expert on aesthetics Luciano Anceschi wrote about Manzoni's "mesmerized surfaces of absolute white, entrusted to the [artist's] sensitivity in the way the material is treated and broken up by plastic reliefs and their shadows." This was Duchamp's idea of "indifférence visuelle" applied to painting; Manzoni was nullifying the idea of "quality" and the dimension of the artifice. The artist's application of material to the canvas was a physical act that remained purely physical, devoid of any aesthetic courtship, and the absence of color—which differs substantially from Yves Klein's concept of the monochrome—producing what Manzoni initially referred to as *Achrome Surfaces*. By giving them this name, Manzoni was indicating the primacy of the physical nature of these works and the objectivity of their surface. Soon Manzoni was using the term *Achrome* to refer to all of his works.

The painting is an elemental physical structure, assumed in all its concreteness, inhabited by visual occurrences that declare their indeterminate presence: appositions, superimpositions, changes in the direction of the material, partitions that are fundamentally insignificant—the horizontal line, the surface divided into squares—produced within the material itself and not superimposed artificially.

The theoretical surface is reabsorbed in the concrete fragments of support soaked in china clay, which solidifies in strong and random sculptural motions whose creases are like signs bearing directions that do not respond to any reason; they enunciate objecthood without implying components of "visibilism," as was the case for almost all the artistic exploration going on in that same period, in Europe as well as in the United States.

For Manzoni, the artwork is a body with a high degree of autonomous objectivity; there is no distinction—whether by reflection or impression—between the body of the artist and the body of the work. Here, the artist's gesture is the essence of the process, not the functional go-between linking the intention and the outcome. The crease is an objective sign, as is the geometric grid that divides the surface into squares. These signs institute a presence, a vision fueled above all by the sense of touch, physically determined yet potentially infinite by way of its indeterminacy. The notion that such indeterminacy carries the stigma of the iteration, of the neutralized multiplication of the same act, asserts the work's quality of nonintentionality, its essence as a project without a destiny or a proposed outcome.

The geometric reverberation of the sign must also be interpreted according to this meaning. Contrary to the rational, metaphysical, knowledge-related moods that the century had broadly distilled, for Manzoni geometry was the source—a profanely ametaphysical one—of being; a minimalization of his process, which focused on art-making without implication, without premeditation, without intention. In the varyingly creased *Achromes*—as well as in those with minimal materiality, in which subdivision was achieved by overlapping portions of the canvas, or directly intervening with neat machine-made stitching—Manzoni focuses on a kind of "materiology." This relates to what Michael Fried would refer to as "the minimal conditions for something's being seen as a painting"—the configuration of a presence that is objectified as a thing among things, but which visibly claims its otherness.

The general form of the *Achrome* corresponds, in the eyes of the viewer, to the rhetorical pattern of the painting, but its substance is pure; it has an unqualified physical presence, reduced to its primary, indifferent essence. The work can thus be an object in itself and, at the same time, an abstract manifestation of thought. Photographs taken in 1959 in Manzoni's studio on Via Fiori Oscuri, Milan, show that the artist was working on a series of works of similar dimensions, reflecting Manzoni's ongoing interest in his works' impressive concrete presence.

In 1959 Leo Paolazzi, a poet and traveling companion of Manzoni's, wrote that the artist's work, "having abolished even the taste for painting, tends to become an object, a desolate presence in itself, with its mesmerizing material (canvas and gesso), the portion of a large white void." When presenting the *Achromes* (accompanied by a statement of intent) in January 1960 in the exhibition *La nuova concezione artistica* at the Azimut Gallery in Milan, Manzoni wrote:

"the question, as far as I'm concerned, is that of rendering a surface that is completely white (actually, colorless and neutral) far beyond the pictorial phenomenon, beyond any intervention extraneous to the value of the surface. A white that is not a polar landscape, nor is it an evocative material or a beautiful one, and neither is it a sensation or a symbol or anything else: just a white surface that is simply that (a colorless surface that is simply a colorless surface). Or rather, a surface that simply is: being (and complete being is pure becoming)."

While the notion of the corporeal can be found in Manzoni's subsequent works—from his *Impronte* (Fingerprints) to his *Sculture viventi* (Living Sculptures) to his *Merda d'artista* (Artist's Shit)—white became a central concept for the artist, detached from any pictorial idiom; evident in his decision to radically alter his approach and exclusively pursue the *Achromes*. Manzoni's use of unconventional materials— from cotton to cloth, to polystyrene, to stones—allowed him to emphasize the immediacy of the *Achromes'* surface; with no element of their form or materiality dictated by pictorial motivations.

PIERO MANZONI
THE TWIN PAINTINGS

ACHROME
ca. 1959
stitched canvas and kaolin
160 × 130 cm / 63 × 51 ⅛ inches

ACHROME
ca. 1959
wrinkled canvas and kaolin
160 × 130 cm / 63 × 51 ⅛ inches

A STORY IN ABSENCE:
MANZONI'S *ACHROMES* AND THE GALERIE SENATORE
Luca Bochicchio

In this essay I will try to trace the history of two major works in Piero Manzoni's oeuvre: two *Achromes* from the collection of the Galerie Senatore, founded in Stuttgart by Pasquale Senatore in 1958. To quote the flawless definition put forward by Rosalia Pasqualino di Marineo in the introduction to this catalogue, the paintings are "heterozygous twins," two large-scale works of the exact same size (160 by 130 centimeters), but different in terms of technique and process of execution: a "creased canvas" and a "sewn canvas," both of which covered in kaolin and dated to around 1959.

Manzoni's exploration of the achrome encompasses all his experimental work as an artist within a circle (an endless one): the *Achromes* made between 1957 and 1958 are in fact the first works to move away from the Nuclear language that had characterized Manzoni's paintings up until then. The year 1957 was crucial: from the point of view of the artist's personal work it was the year when he first made his white paintings (he would start to call them *Achromes* in 1959), but if we widen our gaze to the surrounding historical and cultural context, it was also the year when Manzoni began collaborating with the Movimento Arte Nucleare (Nuclear Art Movement). This movement, founded by Enrico Baj and Sergio Dangelo in 1951, had attracted Manzoni's interest since 1956. Furthermore, during that same period Manzoni was witnessing the development of Lucio Fontana's Spatialism. The artist's participation in the Movimento Arte Nucleare coincides with the publication of the manifesto *Contro lo stile—Contre le style—The End of Style* (1957), which Manzoni signed together with the representatives of the European avant-garde and which implicitly evidenced the surpassing of Nuclear Art.[1] The example set by Alberto Burri, who as early as 1953 had begun working on white paintings and with whom the young Milanese artist became familiar due to publications and the first Milanese exhibition held in January 1957, also contributed to Manzoni's development from Nuclear Art to the self-sufficient use (expressive at first, conceptual later) of material.[2]

Between 1957 and 1958 Piero Manzoni moved from tar (on paper and on canvas) to dull, white, coarse gesso, which he used to cover the canvases of his first white paintings. The concept of the *achrome* (the absence of color) accompanied and supported all of Manzoni's explorations from that moment onwards, until February 1963, when he died prematurely. By experimenting with the use of various materials and supports (from cotton to synthetic fiber, from gesso to kaolin, from everyday objects to natural elements),[3] Manzoni shifts, acquires, and crosses the artistic processes in a conceptual key, revealing not just his alignment with the research that was going on at the same time in the rest of the world, but also the fact that he anticipated and foreshadowed later phases in avant-garde art, from Process Art to Anti-Form.

Although they are contemporary, the works analyzed here derive from two distinct moments in the evolution of the *Achromes*, allowing for a sort of genealogy spanning just three years: initially the canvases were covered in gesso (1957–58), followed by the creased canvases soaked in kaolin (1958–59), and, finally, the sewn canvases that were also covered in kaolin (1959–60);[4] and all of this was naturally characterized by the overlapping, long line of simultaneousness, which other related explorations partook of, such as the *Alfabeti* (Alphabets) from 1958, *Linee* (Lines), *Calendari* (Calendars), and *Corpi d'aria* (Bodies of Air) from 1959.[5]

At the same time that Manzoni was exploring these changes, in March 1958, in the center of Stuttgart, at Charlottenplatz 6, the Galerie Senatore was opening. Its founder, Pasquale Senatore, was born in Salerno, about fifty kilometers south of Naples, in 1921. After joining the navy, he had served in a military submarine during World War II. When the war ended, he studied art conservation, working first in Rome, then in Milan, thus coming into contact with the artistic circles of the early 1950s in Italy's two art capitals, enlightened by two of the brightest stars of the art world, Alberto Burri and Lucio Fontana. Senatore moved to Stuttgart after meeting Maxim Köhler in Vietri. Köhler, who was the director of the Stuttgarter Künstlerbund (Stuttgart Association of Artists), invited Senatore to Germany.[6]

An article by Walter Fedler published in the January 1962 issue of *D'Ars* offers a description of Senatore that tells us about his work as

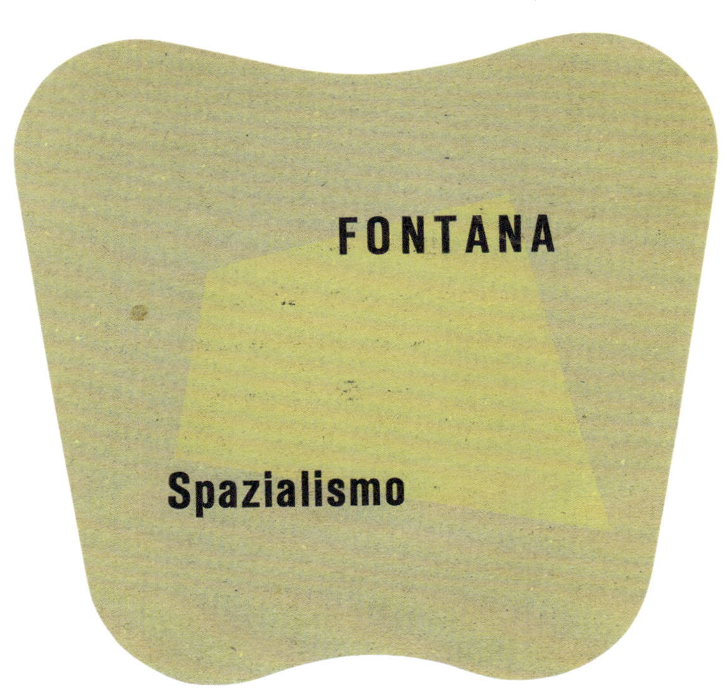

Fig. 1   Invitation to the solo show of the works of Lucio Fontana at the Galerie Senatore,
February 18, 1961

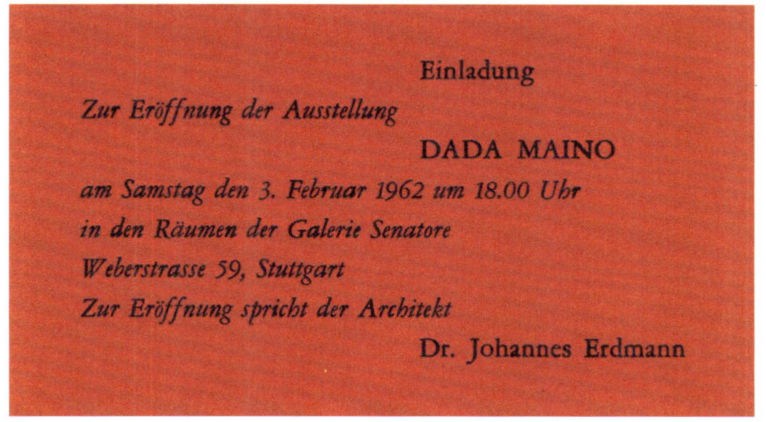

Einladung

Zur Eröffnung der Ausstellung

DADA MAINO

am Samstag den 3. Februar 1962 um 18.00 Uhr

in den Räumen der Galerie Senatore

Weberstrasse 59, Stuttgart

Zur Eröffnung spricht der Architekt

Dr. Johannes Erdmann

Fig. 2   Invitation to the solo show of the works of Dadamaino at the Galerie Senatore, February 3, 1962

an art dealer and gives us some idea about the relationship that may have led to his approach to the work of Manzoni and, later, to his ownership of the two large *Achromes* exhibited here for the first time together.[7]

In Stuttgart, the cultural and social environment that witnessed the founding of the Galerie Senatore does not seem to have been an especially favorable one: both the public and the institutions, which were rather conservative and traditionalist, seem to have been fonder of the Academy and the Opera than of the exploration going on in contemporary art at the time.[8] In 1962 there were only three art galleries to satisfy the tastes of a population of 650,000, and in 1965 the Galerie Lutz & Mayer was forced to close, in spite of its international exhibition activity.[9] Faced with such circumstances, it seems that Senatore knew exactly what he wanted from the very beginning:

"The Galerie Senatore could be reached directly from the street and it was very much like a piece of Montmartre…Senatore's goal, getting people to view the living art of this important century and especially that of his own country, gave him hope that he would make it in Germany…The focus of the exhibitions…is especially on young Italian painters who have not yet made it to the so-called 'market.'"[10]

Pasquale Senatore's determination to pursue exhibition activity that was aimed at contemporary Italian art, the young artists of the Stuttgart Academy, and Chinese and Eastern Art seems to have won out; the art critics at the time said that four years after opening his gallery "he has occupied a permanent place among the German galleries and built a bridge between Italy and southeastern Germany."[11] While working in an environment that was not conducive to the art activity of the time, Senatore remained open to multiple lines of expression and set very few limits of a programmatic nature: "although abstraction prevails, Senatore does not have an exclusive artistic direction. He gives to art, and to all the manifestations the same opportunities."[12] Senatore's aim was to "combine the artistic currents of the time: materials and art objects, lyrical abstraction, reductionism, black and white painting, and the new figuration".[13] At the frenetic pace of about twenty exhibitions per year, until 1960, Senatore exhibited works by artists including Pericle Fazzini, Renato Guttuso, Ibrahim Kodra, and

monochrome malerei

FEBRUAR 1962

maino

GALERIE SENATORE WEBERSTRASSE 59 STUTTGART

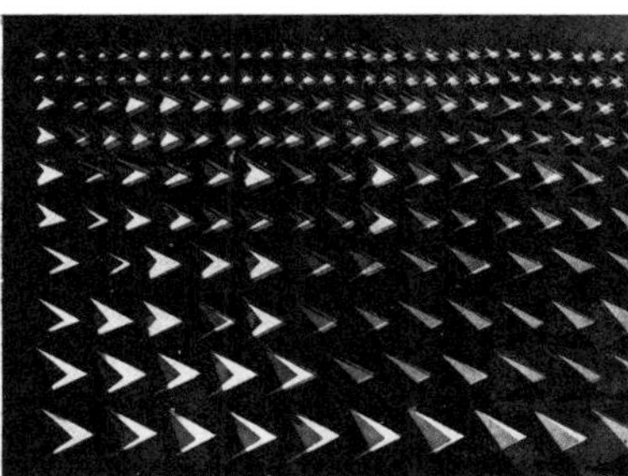

Dada Maino's Malerei gehört der monochromen Tendenz an, welche die Erschaffung einer neuen Dynamik durch leuchtende Vibrationen anstrebt, die durch mehrfache Wiederholung eines gewissen Elementes auf Papier, oder Metall erzielt werden.

Diese Tendenz, zu der in gewisser Hinsicht auch Künstler wie Piene, Mack, Vasarely, Castel ani, Manzoni, Soto und andere zählen, unterscheidet sich eindeutig von gewissen anderen aktuellen; nur scheinbar ähnlichen Strömungen, und zwar von jenen der animierten und multiplizierten Kunst. Während bei jenen Letzteren immer mehr die Neigung besteht, das Kunstwerk in der bisher genehmen Form abzuschaffen, und man häufig bei hinen ein kurioses und nicht immer gerechtfertigtes neodadaistisches Aufbäumen beobachten kann, bleibt bei der monochromen Richtung das Bild als jener abgegrenzte Raum bestehen, auf welchen man eingeladen ist einer Schaustellung beizuwohnen; zwar ist dieser Raum für Beschriftung und Zeichen aufs Minimum reduziert, lässt aber den Künstlern, die uns diese Richtung illustrieren, den Platz für eine Intuition von Licht und Raum frei, die höchst persönlich sein kann.

So im Falle Dada Maino's, we'che Folien in Plastikmaterial übereinanderschichtet und sie mit kreisförmigen, winzigen, wiederholten Löchern versieht. Zum leuchtenden Effekt, zu den vielfältigen Vibrationen gesellt sich, ein Hauch an Chromatismus, der seinen Ursprung in der Art und Weise der Ueberschichtungen des Materiales finder in den fast unwahrnehmbaren Verschiebungen zwischen der einen und anderen Durchlöcherung, die dem Ganzen eine gewisse Tiefenwirkung hinzufügt. Bei ihren letzten Ar-

beiten erlangt Dada Maino eine Dramatisierung ihres expressiven Verfahrens, indem sie das Wiederholungsthema der Plastikfolien betonter isoliert: sie hebt es stark hervor durch die vier aufgeklappten Dreiecklippen, welche die Quadrate bilden, mit denen sie die Oberflächen rythmisch belebt.

Aufmerksam, peinlich genau, bringt Doda Maino mit beherrschter Sensibilität eine zweifellos persönliche Note in ein Forschungsfeld, aus welchem morgen wenigstens ein Teil des zukünftigen ästetischen Glaubensbekenntnis erwachsen kann.

Walter Schönenberger

DADA MAINO ist in Mailand geboren, und hat in Mailand und Paris studiert.
Im Jahre 1956 hat sie zum ersten Male ausgestellt
Sie hat persönliche Ausstel'ungen in Mailand in den Jahren 1958 - 1959 - 1961, in Rom im Jahre 1957 und in Padua im Jahre 1961 veransta'tet.
Gleichzeitig hat sie bei verschiedenen kollektiven Ausstellungen in Italien und im Ausland teilgenommen.
Sie hat an verschiedenen nationalen und internationalen Preisen, zuletzt am XII. Internationale Preis Lissone, ausgestellt
Sie lebt und arbeitet in Mailand.

La pittura di Dada Maino appartiene alla corrente monocroma che tende alla creazione di una nuova dinamica attraverso le vibrazioni luminose prodotte da un elemento ripetuto su un foglio di carta o di metallo. Questa corrente, nella quale rientrano per diversi aspetti artisti come Piene, Mack, Vasarely, Castellani, Manzoni, Soto ecc. si stacca decisamente da altre ricerche attuali, solo apparentemente simili: quelle dell'arte animata e moltiplicata. Mentre in quest'ultime si tende sempre più ad abolire l'opera d'arte, nell'accezione finora avuta, e si assiste a curiose e non sempre giustificabili impennate neododaiste, nella corrente monocroma il quadro rimane quello spazio delimitato in cui si è invitati a partecipare a una finzione, anche se per gli artisti che la stanno attualmente illustrando, la parte lasciata alla scrittura, al segno, si trova ridotta ai minimi termini e lascia il posto a un'intuizione di luce e di spazio che può essere assai personale. Come nel caso di Dada Maino, che sovrappone pellicole di materiale plastico, spesso di diverso colore, e li fora con minuti e ripetuti buchi circolari, All'effetto luminoso, al moltiplicarsi delle vibrazioni, si aggiunge un nuovo, impalpabile cromatismo ricavato dal modo in cui gli strati di materia sono stati sovrapposti, da impercettibili sfasature tra un buco e l'altro che aggiungono un senso di profondità. Nelle sue ultime opere, Dada Maino, ha drammatizzato il suo procedimento espressivo, Isolando maggiormente il tema plastico ripetuto: dandogli un rilievo più evidente coi labbri aperti dei quattro triongoli che compongono i quadrati con cui ritma le sue superfici. Attenta, meticolosa, Dada Maino porta con sorvegliata sensibilità una nota indubbiamente personale in un ordine di ricerche da cui potrà scaturire una parte almeno del credo estetico di domani.

Walter Schönenberger

Fig. 3a–b Frontispiece and inside of the brochure for the solo show of the works of Dadamaino at the Galerie Senatore, 1962

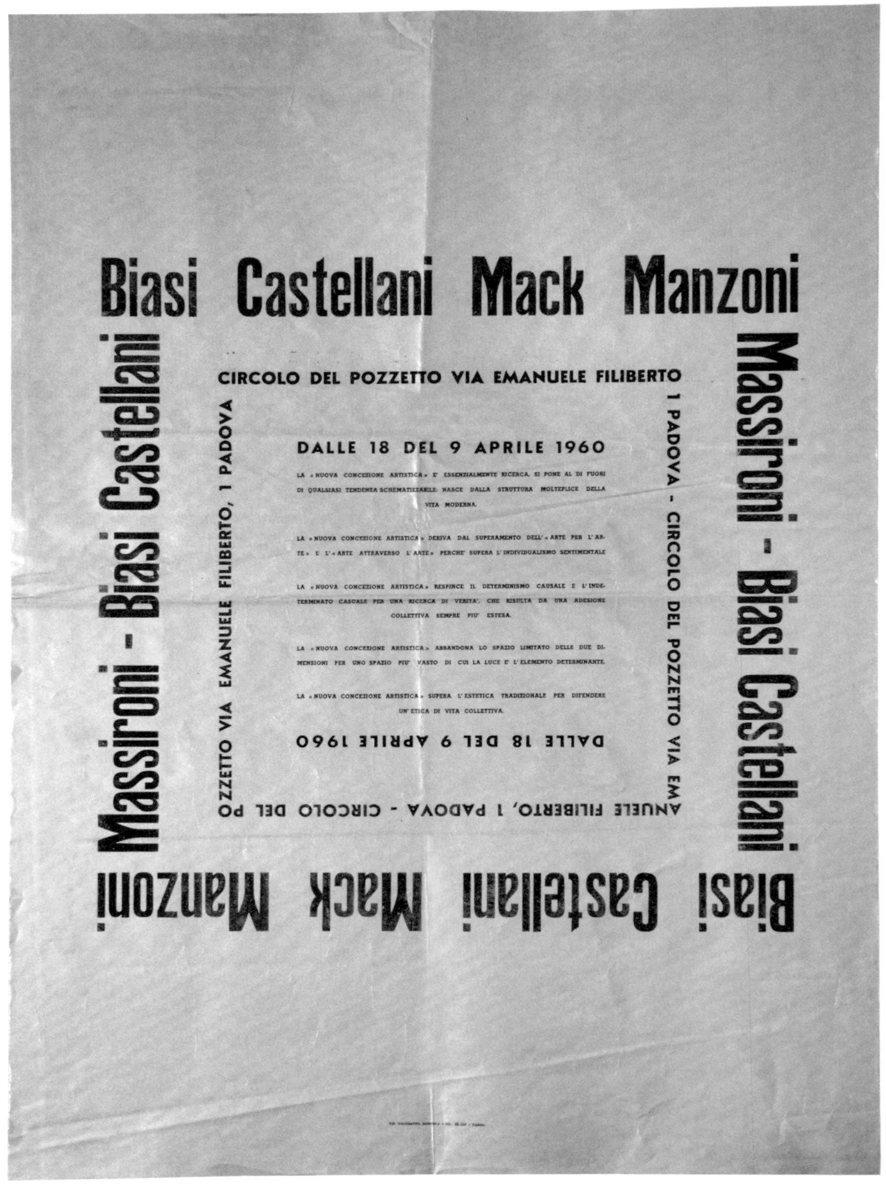

Fig. 4   Poster published on the occasion of the group show *Nuova Concezione Artistica*, 1960

Hsiao Chin. In October 1960 he exhibited Lucio Del Pezzo, in February 1961 Lucio Fontana (fig. 1), and, one year later, Dadamaino (figs. 2–3a): by holding these last three solo shows, and with the presence of Fontana and Heinz Mack in November 1968, Senatore moved in artistic circles that were very close to Piero Manzoni;[14] all the same, Manzoni's works never appeared in the exhibitions of the Stuttgart gallery, not even in the numerous group shows, at least based on what the documentation available tells us.[15]

Another factor concerning any contact there may have been between Manzoni and Senatore—in addition to the northern European artists who were members of the Zero Group, such as Mack, as well as the members of the Milanese avant-garde—is represented by Gruppo 58, the Neapolitan offshoot of the Movimento Arte Nucleare.[16] In the list of exhibitions hosted by the Galerie Senatore and published in the September 1963 issue of *D'Ars* the Gruppo 58 painters Mario Persico and Mario Colucci were described as "gallery artists," thus indicating an ongoing relationship with Pasquale Senatore.[17] Documentation related to this collaboration with the Neapolitan group, which Manzoni was well aware of, and that was constantly in touch with the Milanese movement led by Enrico Baj, can also be found by leafing through the Italian magazine *Documento Sud: Rassegna di arte e di cultura di avanguardia*. The publication, which was based in Naples, brought together poets, critics, and artists both national and international for a platform of research and experimentation, whose purpose was to serve as a cultural stimulus and a point of reference for the avant-garde in southern Italy.[18] In addition to young critics like Enrico Crispolti and Édouard Jaguer, poets like Edoardo Sanguineti, and masters of Art Informel and Abstract Expressionism like Jean Dubuffet and Jackson Pollock, the magazine included articles and the reproductions of the works of artists whom Manzoni knew well: Enrico Baj, Guido Biasi, Mario Colucci, Lucio Del Pezzo, Mario Persico, and Angelo Verga (fig. 4).[19] In 1963 the magazine changed its name to *Linea Sud: Nuova rassegna d'arte e di cultura d'avanguardia*; just as it had in *Documento Sud*, the Galerie Senatore often appeared in the advertising pages that hosted the brands of galleries and magazines referred to by the group (figs. 5–6).

It is thus safe to say that Senatore and Manzoni knew about each other, and although they may not have known each other personally, they were well aware of each other and familiar with each other's work. Further confirmation of this fact can be found in the short text by Walter Schönenberger, published in the catalogue of the Dadamaino show that opened at the Galerie Senatore on February 3, 1962 (fig. 3b):

"Dada Maino's painting belongs to the monochrome current that aims to create a new dynamic via the luminous vibrations produced by an element that is repeated on the sheet of paper or metal. This current, which includes such artists as Piene, Mack, Vasarely, Castellani, Manzoni, Soto, among others, for various reasons, definitely moves away from other contemporary explorations that are only apparently similar; the exploration of art that is animated and multiplied."[20]

To contextualize Dadamaino's work, Schönenberger assimilated his research to that of Manzoni, as well as other artists, distinguishing it from the contemporary experiences of Kinetic and Programmed Art (art that is "animated and multiplied"). It might thus seem strange that Manzoni's works were not even present in the group show dedicated to current trends in Milanese art held in December 1967 at the gallery's new location at Konrad-Adenauer-Strasse 14 (the factory where Schiedmayer pianos used to be manufactured).[21]

Clearly, Pasquale Senatore could not or did not want to add Manzoni to his circuit. And just as we cannot know for sure, at least for now, whether Senatore ever approached or invited Manzoni, we can hypothesize that, because he focused until 1962 on Hsiao Chin, Persico, Del Pezzo, Fontana, and Dadamaino, the art dealer may have entertained the idea of including Manzoni in one of his shows sooner or later. It would be quite logical to imagine Pasquale Senatore being aware of the young Piero Manzoni, but waiting to see what would happen, since it was precisely during the first year of the gallery's activity (1958–59) that the Milanese artist's visual explorations radically changed, and he became immersed in creating *Achromes*.

Although such deductions remain as yet unproven hypotheses, what is instead certain, documented by the "twin" *Achromes* analyzed here, is Pasquale Senatore's interest in Manzoni's work. The

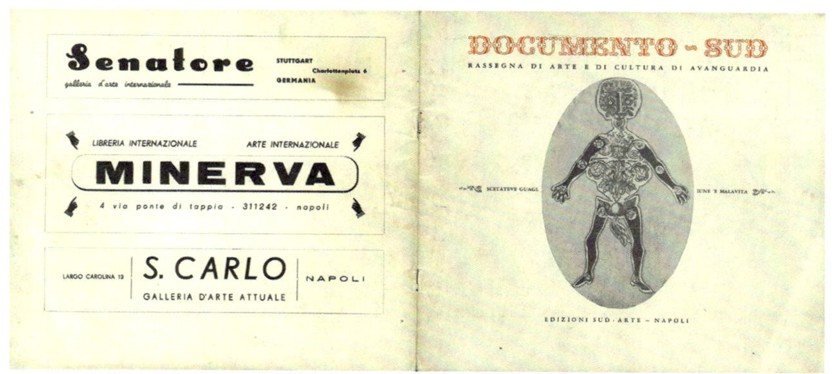

Fig. 5   Cover and back cover of *Documento Sud*, no. 1, 1959, with advertising for the Galerie Senatore

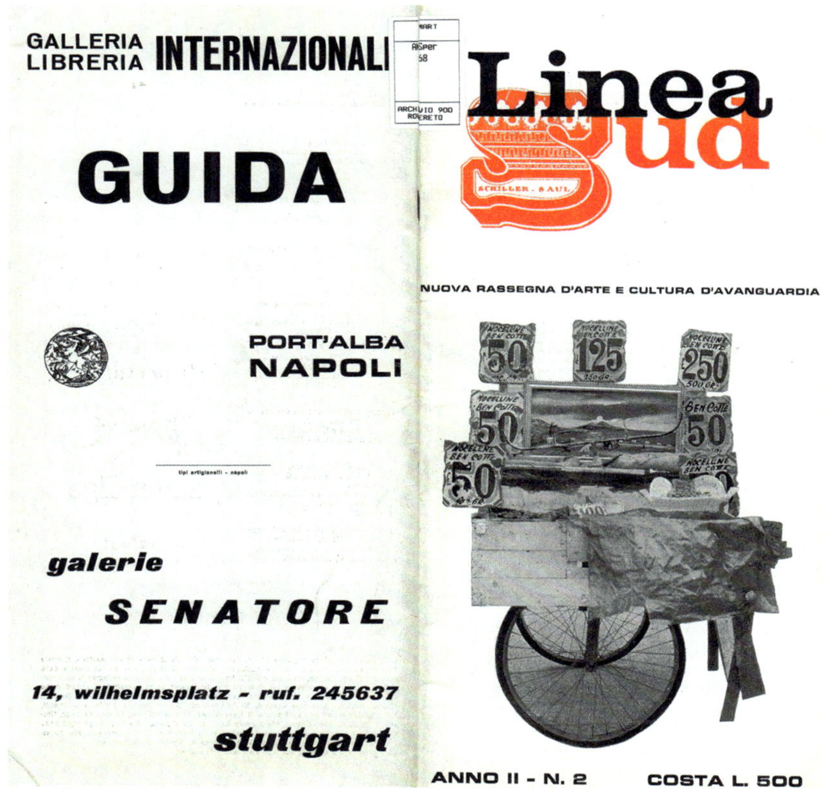

Fig. 6   Cover and back cover of *Linea Sud*, no. 2, 1965, with advertising for the Galerie Senatore

artist's premature death, which may have compromised the chance for the two men to collaborate, does not seem to have prevented the dealer from subsequently acquiring two large *Achromes*.

As concerns the chronology, which is still uncertain, of the Stuttgart art dealer's acquisition of the two works, a letter sent to Pasquale Senatore by Brandstetter & Wyss—Castel Burio Arte, a gallery in Zurich, provides us with a *terminus ante quem* at least for one of them. The letter dated February 26, 1989, reads as follows:

"Dear Pasquale Senatore, I've tried to call you several times but unfortunately to no avail. You told me that you have a Fontana as well as a large work by Manzoni. For both works I have a potential buyer, the owner of Gallerie d'Italia. If you are interested in selling this work, I need you to send me a picture and the standard information (for example, the catalogue number) and the price you're thinking of selling it for, so that I can pass them on. In any case, I was very pleased to hear from you. Warmest wishes, Dani." [22]

The document tells us that Senatore had previously informed Brandstetter & Wyss that he owned both a work by Fontana, and a "large work" (*grosse Arbeit*) by Manzoni.[23] It is likely that the work in question is one of the *Achromes* presented here, which are characterized precisely for their considerable size, as well as for their aesthetic impact.

The fact that Pasquale Senatore considered the works by Manzoni a long-term investment is further proven by the art dealer's brother, who at the start of this century brought the large creased canvas out into the open (after which it was published in Manzoni's *catalogue raisonné* and exhibited in numerous, prestigious venues), stating that Pasquale had recommended he buy it, guaranteeing that the work would prove to be a "safe investment." [24] Indeed, the work bears several stamps by the Galerie Senatore on the verso.

On the other hand, the history of the creased work's twin, the *Achrome* featuring a sewn canvas, is to some extent still shrouded in mystery, and this, perhaps, is what makes all the more interesting.[25] The common ascendancy with respect to the creased canvas is proven both by its rediscovery, in recent years, inside a group of works originally belonging to the Galerie Senatore, and the comparative visual analysis conducted on both paintings: undisputed technical elements confirm that Manzoni made the two paintings at the same time, and in all likelihood for the German collecting circuit, the same circuit that Senatore used to purchase them, probably at some time between the 1970s and the 1980s.

The artist used two identical stretchers to create two works that differed only in the way the materials, which were also identical, were treated: heavy canvas, thin canvas, kaolin. The kaolin that Manzoni used as a visually neutralizing material element is "a pure variety of white clay, [with] an earthy, soft appearance"; as compared with the gesso used by the artist in the early monochrome paintings (1957), this kaolin "is less white, that is, more neutral, more colorless."[26] Both the creased canvas and the sewn one do not "represent" but actually "are" portions of space: "zones of images" that thanks to their structure, to Manzoni's ideational process, tend towards infinity. Hence, the motion of the creases on the canvas—besides beating out the rhythm of the gaze and impressing the body of the painting with space—because of its irregularity escapes the confines of the surrounding frame. Moreover, in the original configuration, the frame is almost a "non-frame": a minimum thickness that allows the viewer to perceive the painting in its purity, as a pure image. Something similar occurs in the sewn canvas, where the *raster* or grid of seams accommodates forty-eight square surfaces, suggesting a unitary, neutral sequence, which solely leads back to itself, to infinity.

From this point of view, the dimension of the two works are anything but a random choice. Manzoni, whose exploration of the body is as important as that of the surface, wanted to affirm here all the power of his theories, establishing a physical presence of the two works, without allowing anything to force him to deviate from the aim he had always set himself: being. And to my mind, the chance to admire these two *Achromes* side by side—something that has never been possible before—without anything else to add to them or distract us, leads to our heightened awareness, to that aesthetic and philosophical radicalness that Manzoni always insisted on and thanks to which his works were and are his determined commitment to share them with the rest of the world.

The dimensions of 160 by 130 centimeters are an ideal size that comes very close to the size of a human being; for this reason as well, when we stand before these two works to gaze at them, we coincide with the image, as if thanks to all the preparatory work done by Manzoni, most of which in a light hue (the veracity of the kaolin layers, the furrowed surfaces in and of themselves), we could remove every degree of separation from being, and could perceive in that moment only ourselves. We identify by reflection in the only surface that does not deceive us, that does not impose on us, that does not guide us: the achrome. Unlike the mirror or the representation, in these two works the very idea of the achrome is affirmed: the source zero of the painting, commonly understood as form, representation, and illusion, fulfilling needs and pressures in style, and taste. Without renouncing the material, the "preparation," Manzoni dismantles all of this, bringing the revolutions triggered by the avant-gardes up until that moment to an extreme. In these twin works, being is duplicated and reiterated, where the medium intersects with the idea. And the change that these two *Achromes* are capable of bringing about in the viewer suddenly sheds light on what the artist wrote in the seminal essay "Per la scoperta di una zona di immagini" (For the Discovery of a Zone of Images; 1958):

"In this way the work of art has the totemic value of living myth … The foundations of the universal value of art are given to us now by psychology. This is the common base that enables art to sink its roots into the origins before man, and to discover the primordial myths of humanity.

"The artist must confront these myths and reduce them, by means of amorphous and confused materials, to clear images.

"Since these are atavistic forces that have their origins in the subconscious, the work of art takes on magical significance. On the other hand, art has always had a religious value, from the first artist-sorcerer to the pagan and Christian myth, etc.… The more we immerse ourselves in ourselves, the more open we become, since the closer we get to the germ of our totality the closer we are to the germ of totality of all men … Images which are as absolute as possible, which cannot be valued for that which they record, explain and express, but only for what they are: being."[27]

1   The manifesto, which was signed in Milan in 1957 by Armand, Enrico Baj, Bemporad, Gianni Bertini, Jacques Colonne, Stanley Chapmans, Mario Colucci, Dangelo, Enrico De Miceli, Reinhout D'Haese, Wout Hoeboer, Hundertwasser, Yves Klein, Théodore Koenig, Piero Manzoni, Nando, Joseph Noiret, Arnaldo Pomodoro, Giò Pomodoro, Pierre Restany, Saura, Ettore Sordini, Serge Vandercam, and Angelo Verga, reads as follows: "Once upon a time Impressionism helped painting get rid of conventional subject-matter; Cubism and Futurism later got rid of the need for the realistic reproduction of objects; and abstraction finally removed the last traces of representational illusion. A new—and final—link today completes this chain: we, nuclear painters, denounce, in order to destroy, the final convention, Style . . . We state that in a world in which the artifices of celebration are rejected, a work of art should be known by the unity of this character, by the effective influence of its appearance and for the simple reality of its living presence."

2   In 1955 the Galleria L'Obelisco published the monographic text on Burri written by James J. Sweeney, the director of the Guggenheim Museum in New York at the time, while the first exhibition of the artist's works in Milan was held at the Il Naviglio gallery from January 12 to 21, 1957. These events are described and carefully documented by Raffaella Perna, *Piero Manzoni e Roma* (Milan: Electa, 2017).

3   For these and other technical elements in the work of Manzoni, see Luisa Mensi, "Naturale, artificiale, sintetico: l'universo dei materiali di Piero Manzoni," in Rosalia Pasqualino di Marineo, ed., *Piero Manzoni: Nuovi studi* (Poggibonsi: Carlo Cambi, 2017), 11–25.

4   This chronological distribution is not only based on the *catalogue raisonné* of the work of Manzoni, but is reconstructed by the artist himself in an unpublished typewritten text (now included in Gaspare Luigi Marcone, ed., *Piero Manzoni: Scritti sull'arte* [Milan: Abscondita, 2013], 89–90). In it, speaking about himself in the third person, he states that: "In 1957 he began the achrome movement with white paintings, at first made of gesso canvas and glue ('57–'59) then in sewn canvas ('59–'60), then in fur, or cotton, or synthetic fibers ('61–'62)." The main explicatory texts subsequently published by Manzoni confirm that the achromes first began in 1957, overlooking the intermediate phase involving gesso: "My first 'achromes' are dated to '57: in canvas soaked in kaolin and glue: since '59 the *raster* of the 'achromes' consists of machine-made stitches." Piero Manzoni, "I miei primi 'achromes' sono del '57," *Evoluzione delle lettere e delle arti* (Milan), I, 1, January 1963, 49, now in Marcone, *Piero Manzoni: Scritti sull'arte*, 50–52.

5   See Flaminio Gualdoni and Rosalia Pasqualino di Marineo, eds., *Piero Manzoni 1933–1963*, exh. cat. (Milan: Palazzo Reale, March 26–June 2, 2014; with Milan: Skira, 2014); Germano Celant, *Piero Manzoni: Catalogo generale* (Milan: Skira, 2004).

6   Information and documentation about Pasquale Senatore and the Galerie Senatore can be consulted in fond 2179 of the Stadtarchiv in Stuttgart, which also contains the unpublished biographical document *Spuren-sicherung mit vertauschten Rollen: Galerie Senatore—ein Rückblick*, 1979 (document no. 196).

7   Walter Fedler, "Pasquale Senatore," *D'Ars*, I, III, 1 (1962), 15.

8   "The cultural environment gave him very few chances to resist for long in a town as traditional as the capital of Wurttemberg. In recent years, many Galleries had come and gone . . . What mostly counted in Stuttgart's artistic life were the auctions held at the Ketterer [and] so Stuttgart does not have a wealth of private galleries, and the ones it does have do not easily engage with modern painting that isn't of a very high level . . . Owing to their spiritual laziness, many viewers remain attached to their past and to tradition, and it is for this reason that the issue of contemporary art can be problematic. Against all the new, unproven attempts still to be demonstrated, until now the Galleries have clashed with scathing criticism." Fedler, "Pasquale Senatore."

9   "After the death of Otto Lutz (1962)—the last owner of the Gallery—the Lutz & Meyer, under a new administration, had found Willi Schoeningh to be a good director; the member of a family of publishers from Westphalia, he had managed to expand the gallery's activity, introducing the important participation of foreign artists [:] Robert Helman, . . . Adams, Cooper, Davie, Hepworth, Nicholson, Scott, . . . Music, Cimiotti, Appel, Van Der Steen, Serpan, Friedlaender, Giorgio Morandi . . ." Walter Fedler, "A Stoccarda si è chiusa la galleria Lutz & Meyer," *D'Ars*, I, IV, 1 (1965), 153.

10   Fedler, "Pasquale Senatore."

11   Ibid.

12   Ibid.

13   *Spurensicherung mit vertauschten Rollen: Galerie Senatore—ein Rückblick*, 1979 (document no. 196, fond 2179 of the Stadtarchiv in Stuttgart).

14   It is commonly known that Manzoni and Lucio Fontana both held each other in esteem. The two artists exhibited their work in a group show that also included Enrico Baj in Bergamo (Galleria Bergamo, January 4–17, 1958) and Bologna (Galleria del Circolo di Cultura, March 23–April 8, 1958). On the relationship between Manzoni and Heinz Mack and the Gruppo Zero, see Francesca Pola, *Piero Manzoni e ZERO: Una regione creativa europea* (Milan: Electa, 2014); more in general, for the European network, see Flaminio Gualdoni, *Piero Manzoni: Vita d'artista* (Milan: Johan & Levi, 2013); Luca Massimo Barbero, ed., *Azimut/h: Continuità e nuovo* (Venice: Marsilio, 2014).

15   A copy of the list of exhibitions held at the Galerie Senatore from 1958 to 1973 (the original is in the fond for Pasquale Senatore of the Stadtarchiv in Stuttgart) is preserved in the archive of the Fondazione Piero Manzoni, Milan.

16   See "Piero Manzoni ha collaborato all'attività del Movimento Arte Nucleare nel 1957," in Marcone, *Piero Manzoni: Scritti sull'arte*, 74–75. On the developments in the Movimento Arte Nucleare, including relations with Piero Manzoni and the Gruppo 58, see Elio Santarella, ed., *Arte Nucleare 1951–1957: Opere – testimonianze – documenti*, exh. cat. (Milan: Galleria San Fedele, with Comune di Milano, 1980).

17   "Notiziario. Dalla Germania. Stoccarda," *D'Ars*, I, IV, 5, 1963, 131.

18   *Documento Sud* and *Linea Sud* are available in the online data bank "CAPTI Contemporary Art Periodicals Texts Illustrations."

19   Together with Alberto Biasi, Mario Colucci, Ettore Sordini, and Angelo Verga, Manzoni signed the so-called *Manifesto di Albissola Marina*, published on the occasion of the group show from August 1 to 15, 1957, probably in the Trattoria da Lalla in Albissola Marina (Savona). On the occasion of the group show *Nuova Concezione Artistica* (Circolo del Pozzetto, Padua), which opened on April 9, 1960, Manzoni published along with Biasi, Enrico Castellani, Heinz Mack, and Manfredo Massironi the eponymous programmatic text, reproduced here (fig. 4). On Manzoni's presence in Albisola, see Francesca Pola, *Una visione internazionale: Piero Manzoni e Albisola* (Milan: Electa, 2013).

20   Walter Schönenberger, *Dada Maino: Monochrome Malerei* (Stuttgart: Galerie Senatore, February 1962).

21   Manzoni's name is not even included in the graphic scheme that traces an abstract plan of the artistic points of reference on the Milanese art scene, contained in the previously mentioned list of exhibitions held at the Galerie Senatore from 1958 to 1973 (see note 15). This scheme—which may have been taken from a document produced by the gallery, or it may have been created later by the person who compiled the study on Senatore—includes the following names: "Fontana," "Gruppo Cibernetico: Parini, Casadei," "Poesia Visuale: Balestrini, Isgrò, Vaccari," "Gruppo T: Colombo, Boriani, De Vecchi, Variso," and then in the orbit albeit independent: "Castellani, Enzo Mari, Munari," "Fabro, Pizzo Greco, Del Ponte," "Marzot, Nigro, Edival Ramosa, Vigo."

22   The original in German reads as follows: "Lieber Pa[s]quale Senatore, Ich habe mehrmals versucht, Sie telefonisch zu erreichen, leider immer ohne Erfolg. Wie Sie mir sagten, besitzen Sie einen Fontana und auch eine grosse Arbeit von Manzoni. Für beide Werke habe ich einen möglichen Interessenten, einen Galeristen aus Italien. Falls fur Sie ein Verkauf dieser Arbeiten in Frage kommen sollte, bitte ich Sie mir ein Foto und die üblichen Angaben (Ev. Werkverzeichnis-Nr.) und Ihre Preisvorstellungen zukommen zu lassen, damit ich sie weiterleiten kann. In jedem Falle würde ich mich sehr freuen von Ihnen zu hören. Herzliche Grüsse, Dani." A copy of the letter, preserved at the Stadtarchiv in Stuttgart, is available in the archive of the Fondazione Piero Manzoni, Milan.

23   The letter was written after the Galerie Senatore was closed. According to what is reported in the biography contained in the archive in Stuttgart, after the death of his wife in a car accident, on December 9, 1985, Pasquale Senatore retired to Italy and died in Gaeta in 2000.

24   The work is catalogued under no. 192 in Celant, *Piero Manzoni: Catalogo generale*, *Tomo primo,* 111; *Tomo secondo,* 423. It is also published in the following volumes and exhibitions catalogues: Luca Massimo Barbero, ed., *Informale: Jean Dubuffet e l'arte europea 1945–1970* (Modena: Foro Boario and Venice: Peggy Guggenheim Collection, Milan: Skira, 2005); Gabriella Belli, ed., *Italia nova: Une aventure de l'art talien 1900–1950* (Paris: Galeries Nationales du Grand Palais, with Milan: Skira and Paris: Réunion des Musées Nationaux, 2006); Germano Celant, ed., *Piero Manzoni* (Naples: MADRE Museo d'Arte Contemporanea Donnaregina; with Milan: Electa, 2007); Germano Celant, ed., *Manzoni* (New York: Gagosian Gallery, with Milan: Skira, 2009); Martin Engler, ed., *Piero Manzoni: Als Körper Kunst wurden* (Frankfurt am Main: Städel Museum, with Bielefeld and Berlin: Kerber Verlag, 2013); Germano Celant, *Su Piero Manzoni* (Milan: Abscondita, 2014); Daniela Ferrari, ed., *Oltre il confine della tela: Fontana, Burri, Manzoni, Dadamaino, Bonalumi, Scheggi* (Riva del Garda: MAG Museo Alto Garda, 2015).

25   Work archived by the Fondazione Piero Manzoni under the number 1373A/14.

26   Mensi, "Naturale, artificiale, sintetico," 19.

27   Piero Manzoni, "Per la scoperta di una zona di immagini," in *Documenti d'arte d'oggi mac 58* (Milan: Libreria Salto Editrice, 1958), 74; also published in Marcone, *Piero Manzoni: Scritti sull'arte*, 25–27.

Achrome, ca. 1959, stitched canvas and kaolin (detail)

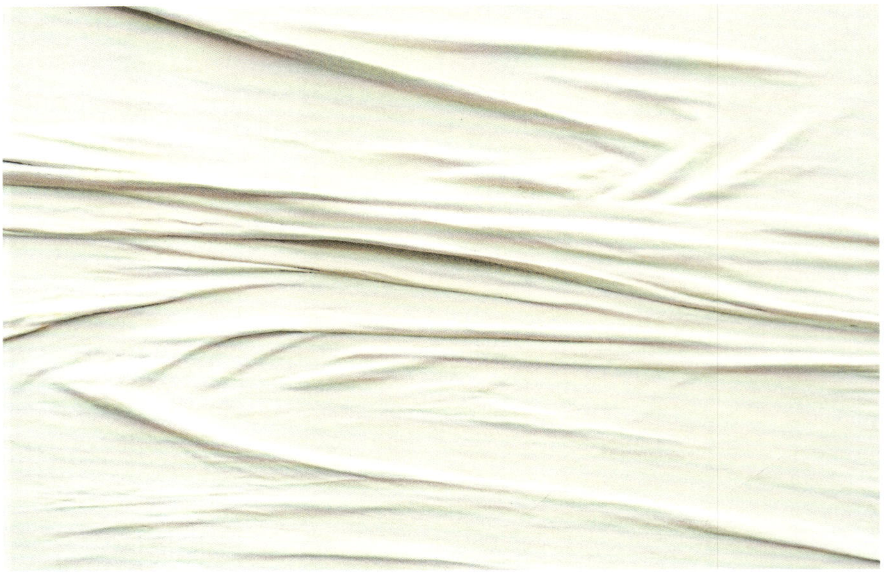

Achrome, ca. 1959, wrinkled canvas and kaolin (detail)

PROPAGATION. PROLIFERATION. EXPANSION.
Luisa Mensi

The American art critic Harold Rosenberg, who was the first in the 1950s to use the term "action" in relation to painting practice,[1] wrote in his 1969 essay "Art and Words" published in the *New Yorker*: "A contemporary painting or sculpture is a species of centaur—half art materials, half words. The words are the vital, energetic element, capable, among other things, of transforming any materials (epoxy, light beams, string, rocks, earth) into art materials."[2] In the work of Piero Manzoni it seems that the scale is tipped more toward concepts and words, although this is not necessarily definitive. Manzoni's concept of *Achromes* stemmed from his idea to express and "inflect" a minimal, absolute concept that was absolutely devoid of color, which he applied in his all-encompassing survey of natural and man-made things.

The *Achrome*, which propagates infinitely between the creases of a cotton canvas—easily manipulated, especially when wet—or amid the multiple repetitions of stitching, is reminiscent of the seams of several pieces of canvas that were sewn together to create large-scale paintings, the so-called *teleri,* that were typical of Renaissance Venice. Venetian painters used such seams to expand and dilate the pictorial space to fill the architectural space, transcending the limits of the canvas's width that was determined by the breadth of the weaver's gesture.

Although in the past the seam was deftly concealed among the pictorial elements of the composition, it is clearly visible in Manzoni's work, and it is even accentuated, thus bestowing physical presence, relief, and rhythm on the measurement of space. The rhythmic measurement of space in the canvases sewn by Manzoni also alludes to the grid used by artists—both ancient and modern—in preparatory drawings or cartoons so they could accurately transfer, or have others transfer, an enlarged version of the subject to a wall, tapestry, or large-scale canvas. This reference thus prompts the physical and mental dilatation of the work in the eye and in the imagination of the beholder.

It is possible that these twin works—two large-scale canvases created in the same place and at the same time—were commissioned together. Such a hypothesis is suggested by the appearance of the works. Not only are they identical in shape and dimension; they are also mounted on identical stretchers. The canvas of their supports is identical, as is visible on the reverse. The works are both finished along the edges with a strip of enamel-painted wood, and the space between the wood and the canvas is filled in, as if to say that the work does not end there but, instead, continues. The material covering both canvases is identical, even though it has been laid down differently. Details in execution that both works share nevertheless differ from most of Manzoni's oeuvre. While the creases were smoothed by the application of the impasto over the surface, the seams were emphasized by a series of markings made by reworking the surface with crossed brushstrokes of impasto and then engraving the lines of the stitching when the impasto was still fresh.

Although at a quick glance they might all appear to be the same, Manzoni's technique varied to such an extent that each work is different: thick canvas underneath and thin canvas on top, or thin canvas underneath and thick canvas on top, impasto applied to soften the roughness of the creases, or marks to accentuate the lines. Materials are thus used in many different ways, and many different materials are used, including materials that differ in the chromatic shade of whites, while remaining similar—similar, yet not identical.

Manzoni alternatively used kaolin, calcium sulfate, calcium carbonate, polystyrene, cotton fabric, cotton wool, and felt for the final, top layer of his *Achrome;* these are all materials that convey the idea of the absence of color and of neutrality. The intermediate layer of the priming, which is executed using various types of gesso and then covered with paint, is characteristically neutral in nineteenth- and twentieth-century academic painting, not influencing the tone. It is also found in the intermediate layer of polychrome ceramics, especially pottery made of terra-cotta, which is coated with a colloidal suspension of kaolin.

"We want the evolution of art by means of the medium,"[3] wrote Lucio Fontana in 1966, on the reverse of one of his famous *Tagli* (Slashes), in a single sentence summarizing what he had already stated in his manifestos from the 1940s and 1950s.[4] Contained in his use of the word "we" is all the sentiment of a generation of artists who paid new attention to looking for new materials to make art, actually as a catalyst for artistic evolution. The "we" also embraces all his "travel companions" including artists who were considerably younger than himself, artists whom he admired, encouraged, and supported. Among them was Piero Manzoni, who had died a few years before, but who had succeeded in turning that statement into his artistic practice.

1   Harold Rosenberg coined the term "action painting" in the 1950s, stressing the importance of the gesture in painting.

2   Harold Rosenberg, "Art and Words," *The New Yorker,* March 29, 1969, 110.

3   Lucio Fontana, inscription on the reverse of *Concetto spaziale: Attese,* 1966, private collection. The original Italian reads "Noi vogliamo l'evoluzione dell'arte attaverso il mezzo."

4   Enrico Crispolti, *Lucio Fontana: Catalogo ragionato di sculture, dipinti, ambientazioni* (Milan: Skira, 2006), vol. I, 111–14, 116–18. With this statement Fontana reiterated what he had already expressed in the *Manifesto Blanco* (White Manifesto) of 1946, whose subtitle was *Noi continuiamo l'evoluzione dell'arte* (We Are Continuing the Evolution of Art); in the *Proposta di un regolamento Movimento spaziale* (Proposal for Regulations Spatial Movement) in 1950, of which point four declares: "The great revolution of the Spatialists lies in the evolution of the medium in art"; and in the *Manifesto tecnico dello spazialismo* (Technical Manifesto of Spatialism) of 1951, whose main title is *Noi continuiamo l'evoluzione del mezzo nell'arte* (We Are Continuing the Evolution of the Medium in Art).

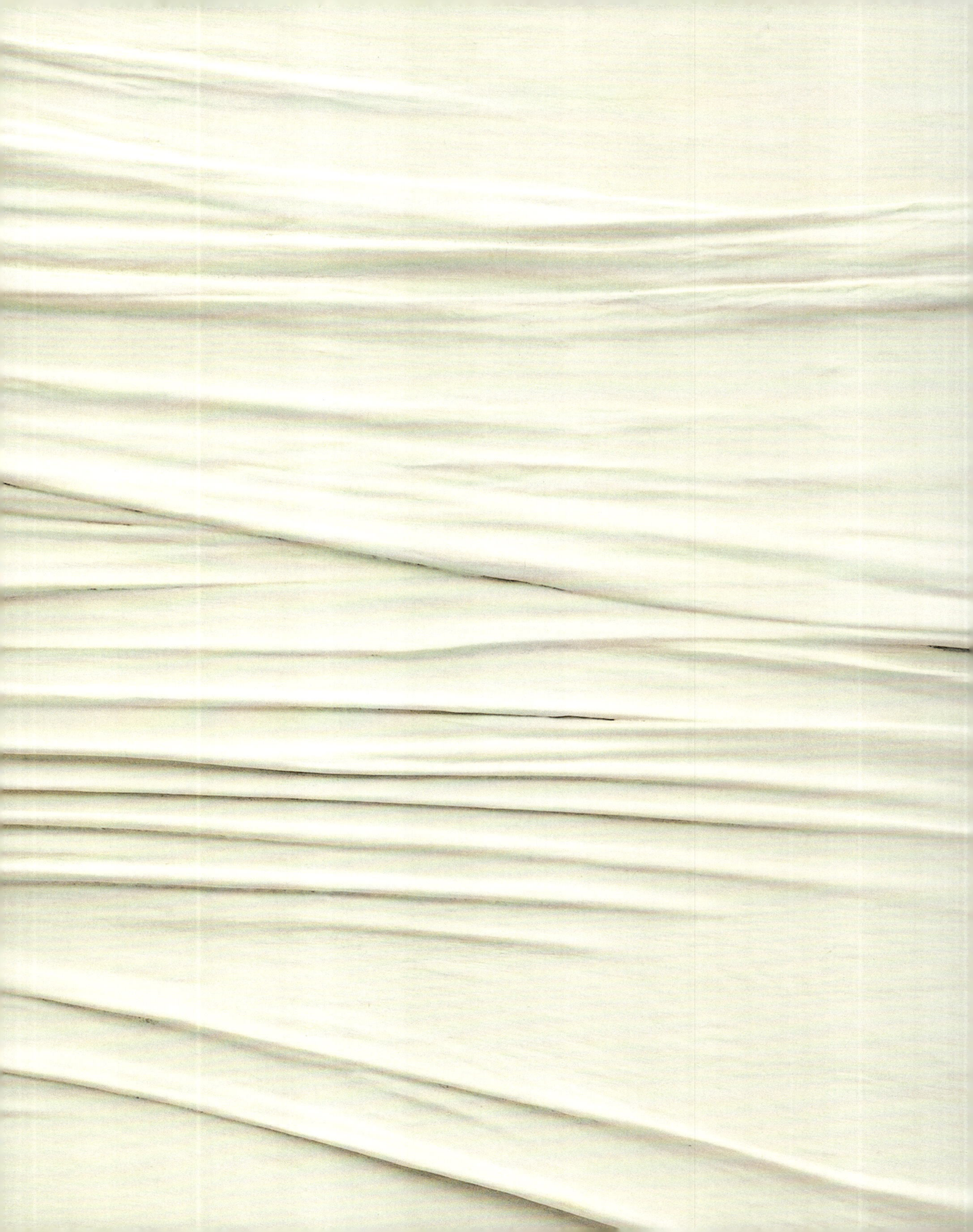

BIOGRAPHY: PIERO MANZONI

Piero Manzoni was born in Soncino, Cremona, Italy on July 13, 1933. After earning a diploma at the Istituto Leone XIII, a Jesuit classical lyceum, he intermittently attended the Faculty of Law and the Faculty of Philosophy. For many years, he spent his summers in Albissola, a holiday resort town in Liguria and a rendezvous for many artists from Asger Jorn to Lucio Fontana.

In 1956 Manzoni debuted as an artist at the 4a Fiera mercato: Mostra d'arte contemporanea hosted by the Castello Sforzesco in Soncino, and a few months later he showed his works at the Premio di pittura San Fedele in Milan. During those years he made paintings featuring anthropomorphic silhouettes and the impressions of objects. His artistic activity intensified, and he began participating in group shows and signing manifestos alongside other artists, including Enrico Baj, Guido Biasi, Ettore Sordini, and Angelo Verga. For a period of time he embraced the Movimento Arte Nucleare, but abandoned it early in 1958.

In late 1957 he began making his first "white paintings," later named *Achromes*, at first with rough gesso, and then with kaolin, as well as canvases with creases or a surface divided into squares. On several occasions he showed his work with Agostino Bonalumi and Enrico Castellani, and he began to collaborate with the artists in the Zero Group in Düsseldorf and other European neo-avant-garde groups, continuing to do so in the years that followed. In 1959 the Galleria Azimut in Milan opened with an exhibition of Manzoni's *Linee* (Lines). Manzoni and Castellani promoted the gallery, just as they did the magazine *Azimuth*, of which only two issues were published. Agostino Bonalumi, Enrico Castellani, Gianni Colombo, Dadamaino, Gabriele Devecchi, Yves Klein, Heinz Mack, Almir Mavignier, and Günther Uecker were among those who showed their work at the Galleria Azimuth. The second issue of *Azimuth* (1960) included the essay "Libera dimensione" (Free Dimension), one of Manzoni's seminal texts. In 1959 the artist began creating the series of *Corpi d'aria* (Bodies of Air), an inflated white balloon set on a tripod, followed in 1960 by *Fiato d'artista* (Artist's Breath), an inflated balloon set on a wooden plinth. Manzoni spent the summer of 1960 in Herning, Denmark, where—thanks to the patronage of Aage Damgaard—he was able to make several works, experimenting with unconventional materials. One of the works he made was *Linea di 7200 m* (7200-Meter Line). While continuing to produce *Achromes* in cotton, phosphorescent polystyrene, and cobalt chloride, Manzoni designed the *Placentarium*, "a pneumatic theater for ballets of light, gas, etc." and in July 1960 he presented *Consumazione dell'arte/dinamica del pubblico/divorare l'arte* (Consumption of Art by the Art-Devouring Public) in Milan, an event during which he offered the public hard-boiled eggs with his thumbprint on them. This was the last event seen at the Azimut. In parallel with new cycles of *Achromes* (in fiberglass and synthetic fiber, rabbit skin, bread, straw, and wrapping paper), in 1961 Manzoni began signing actual people, turning them into "living sculptures," and awarding them with a certificate of authenticity. He made "magic bases" and ninety cans of *Merda d'artista* (Artist's Shit), "30 grams, dried naturally," exhibited for the first time in Albissola. On the occasion of his second stay in Herning, in 1961, he presented *Base del Mondo* (The Base of the World), an upside-down metal plinth ideally holding up the world as though it were a work of art. Manzoni participated in many solo and group shows in private galleries and in avant-garde spaces both in Italy and abroad (Albissola, Bern, Brussels, Copenhagen, Düsseldorf, London, Rome, Rotterdam, Taipei, Zagreb) but also at institutional venues (for example, the group shows *Monochrome Malerei*, Städtisches Museum, Leverkusen, 1960; *Contemporary Italian Art*, Illinois Institute of Design, Chicago, 1960; and *Tentoonstelling Nul*, Stedelijk Museum, Amsterdam, 1962). During those years Manzoni also filmed some of his cycles ("lines," "living sculptures," "bodies of air," and "eggs"). Around 1961–62 Manzoni and with the publisher Jes Petersen planned a "monographic text" with totally transparent pages. In 1962 Vanni Scheiwiller published Manzoni's *8 Tavole d'accertamento* (8 Plates of Assessment) accompanied by a text written by Vincenzo Agnetti. Manzoni continued to produce *Achromes* made of cotton balls, stones, and polystyrene pellets.

On February 6, 1963, Manzoni suffered a fatal heart attack in his studio on Via Fiori Chiari, Milan.

CONTRIBUTOR BIOGRAPHIES

Luca Bochicchio

Luca Bochicchio is an Italian art historian, critic, and curator, focusing on modern and contemporary art. He is the artistic director of the Asger Jorn House Museum, Albissola, Italy, and since 2011, has been curator at the Museo Diffuso Albissola. He obtained his PhD in Arts, Theater, and Multimedia Technologies at the University of Genoa, where he is currently a lecturer in New Media Art and teaching assistant in Contemporary Art. He is the author of books, articles, and catalog essays focusing on topics such as post-human culture, ceramics in contemporary art, cultural heritage, Asger Jorn, Enrico Baj, Leoncillo, Futurism, and nineteenth-century Italian sculpture.

As an art critic he is a regular contributor to the Italian magazines *Espoarte* and *La Ceramica,* and has curated exhibitions for museums and private institutions in Italy and abroad.

Flaminio Gualdoni

Flaminio Gualdoni is professor of Art History at the Accademia di Belle Arti di Brera in Milan. He is the former director the Galleria Civica in Modena, Musei Civici in Varese, and the Fondazione Arnaldo Pomodoro in Milan. Notable recent publications include *Il corpo delle immagini, immagini del corpo: Tableaux vivants da san Francesco a Bill Viola* (Monza, 2017), *Breve storia della "Merda d'artista"* (Milan, 2014), and *Piero Manzoni: Vita d'artista* (Monza, 2013).

Luisa Mensi

Luisa Mensi works in the conservation, restoration, and study of works of contemporary art. She regularly collaborates with the Castello di Rivoli—Museum of Contemporary Art, Turin; Le Stanze del Vetro, Fondazione Giorgio Cini, Venice; Fondazione Giulio e Anna Paolini, Turin; Fondazione Piero Manzoni, Milan; Grimaldi Forum, Monte Carlo; and AXA ART Italia. Mensi teaches history of artistic technique at the Università IUAV di Venezia, Venice. She also collaborates with Palazzo Grassi, Punta della Dogana, Venice; Fondazione Giovanni e Marella Agnelli, Pinacoteca del Lingotto; Galleria d'Arte Moderna e Contemporanea, Turin; Garage Museum, Moscow; and Fondazione Pistoletto, Cittadellarte, Biella. Mensi has participated in conferences in Italy and abroad as well as published articles and essays on topics related to the conservation and restoration of contemporary artworks.

Piero Manzoni: The Twin Paintings
Published by Hauser & Wirth Publishers and Fondazione Piero Manzoni

The Fondazione Piero Manzoni would like to thank: Archivio del '900 at MART Museo d'arte moderna e contemporanea di Trento e Rovereto, Luca Bochicchio, Agnese Boschini, Sara Danese, Cristiano and Fabrizio Cairati, Duccio Dogheria, Dino Facchini, Fondazione Lucio Fontana, Paolo Giubileo, Flaminio Gualdoni, Kristina Hinrichsen, Heike van der Horst, Nini Laurini, Luisa Mensi, Daniela Migotto, Beatriz Millar, Cecilia Nelli, Sylvia Notini, Marc Payot, Fiona Römer, Zacharias Sautner, Karin Seinsoth, Irene Stucchi, Stadtarchiv Stuttgart, Michaela Unterdörfer, Maria Villa, and Iwan and Manuela Wirth.

Editor: Rosalia Pasqualino di Marineo
Project: Fiona Römer, Karin Seinsoth
Editorial coordination: Kristina Hinrichsen
Design and typography: Vera Kaspar and Huber-Sterzinger
Translations: Sylvia Notini
Copyediting and proofreading: Emma Capps, Tas Skorupa
Production coordination: Christine Stäcker
Pre-press: Jan Scheffler, prints professional, Berlin
Production: Offsetdruckerei Karl Grammlich GmbH, Pliezhausen/
Josef Spinner Grossbuchbinderei GmbH, Ottersweier

Piero Manzoni: The Twin Paintings
Achrome, ca. 1959, stitched canvas and kaolin, 160 × 130 cm / 63 × 51 ⅛ inches (p. 14, details: pp. 2–3, 32–33)
Achrome, ca. 1959, wrinkled canvas and kaolin, 160 × 130 cm / 63 × 51 ⅛ inches, private collection
(p. 15, details: pp. 38–39, 46–47)

Photo Credits
pp. 2–3, 14, 15, 32–33, 38–39, 46–47: Jon Etter; p. 8: Ennio Vicario

Copyright Credits
p. 19 (fig. 1): © Fondazione Lucio Fontana, Milan; p. 19 (fig. 2), p. 21 (figs. 3a–b): © Archivio Dadamaino, Somma Lombardo, Varese; p. 22 (fig. 4): © Fondazione Piero Manzoni, Milan; p. 25 (figs. 5, 6): © Archivio del '900, fondo librario Martini, MART, Rovereto

Available in North America through
ARTBOOK | D.A.P.
75 Broad Street, Suite 630
New York, NY 10004
Tel 212 627 1999 | Fax 212 627 9484

ISBN 978-3-906915-13-5

Printed and bound in Germany

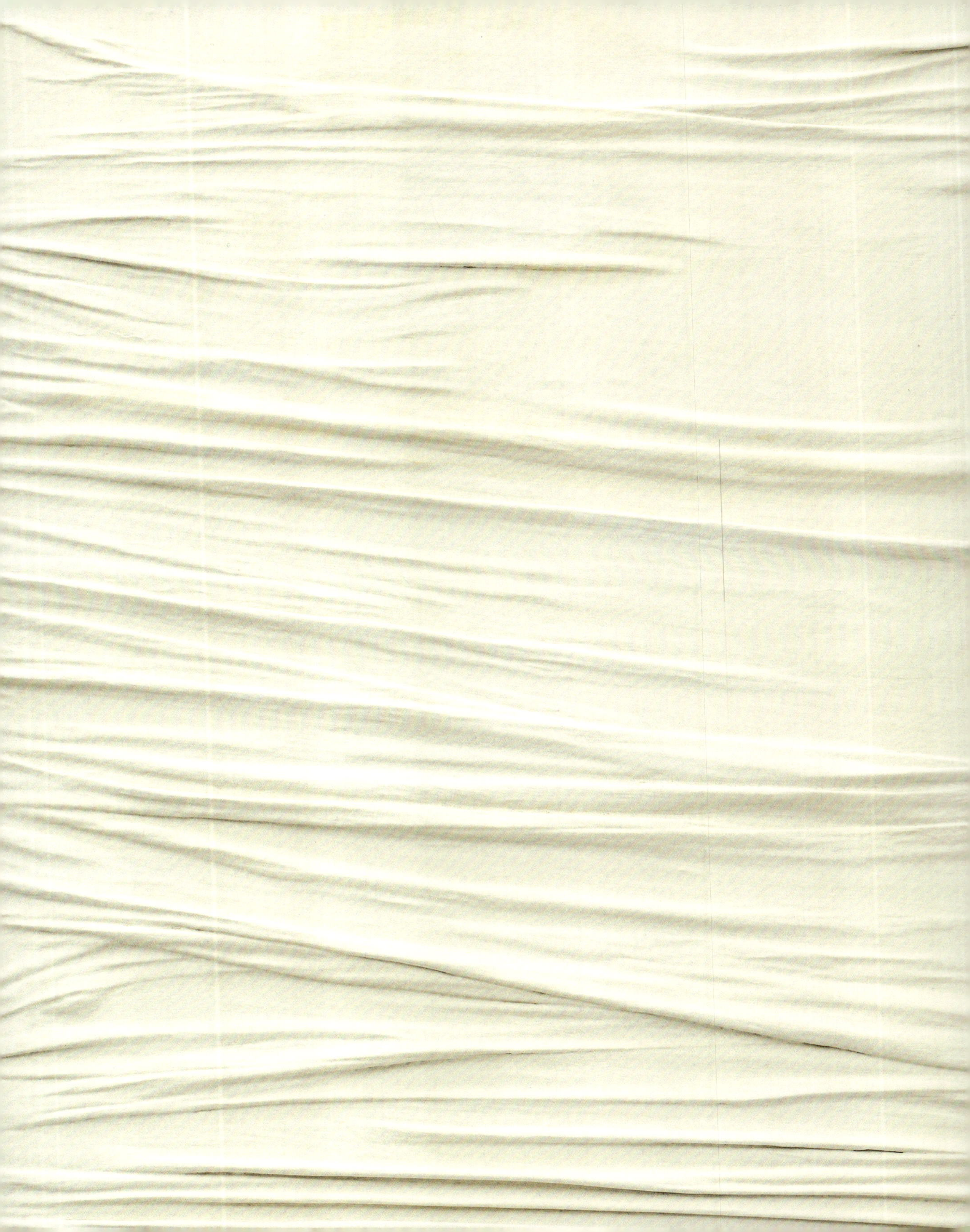